P9-BYK-299

GROVER'S BOOK OF CUTE LITTLE BABY ANIMALS

By B. G. Ford
Illustrated by Tom Leigh

A SESAME STREET/READER'S DIGEST KIDS BOOK

Published by Reader's Digest Young Families, Inc.,
in cooperation with Children's Television Workshop

© 1992, 1980 Children's Television Workshop. Jim Henson's Sesame Street Muppet Characters © 1992 Jim Henson Productions, Inc. All rights reserved. Unauthorized reproduction, in any manner, is prohibited. Printed in the U.S.A. SESAME STREET, the SESAME STREET SIGN, and the SESAME STREET BOOK CLUB are trademarks and service marks of Children's Television Workshop. READER'S DIGEST KIDS & DESIGN is a registered trademark of The Reader's Digest Association, Inc.
ISBN: 0-89577-702-9

Photo Credits: From ANIMALS ANIMALS: p. 10 © Z. Leszcynski; p. 11 © Michael & Barbara Reed; p. 12 © Charles Palek 1978; p. 13 top © Gary W. Griffin; pp. 14-15 © Roger Minkoff; p. 16 © L.L.T. Rhodes; p. 17 © Margot Conte; p. 19 © Dagmar; p. 22 © M. Austerman; p. 23 © Tanaka Kojo; p. 24 © Fran Allan; p. 25 © Charles Palek; p. 26 © Fran Allan. Courtesy THE BETTMANN ARCHIVE: p. 13 bottom. From PHOTO RESEARCHERS, INC.: p. 18 © Elisabeth Weiland; pp. 20-21 © Edmund Appel.

Sh-h-h-h!

Oh, I am so excited! I am going to borrow a book from the library.

QUIET PLEASE

Baby cats are called kittens.
Kittens have soft fur and sharp claws.
When kittens are happy, they purr.

Baby dogs are called puppies.
They love to run and bark and play.
Kittens and puppies make good pets.

Oh, my goodness.
They are so cute
and furry!

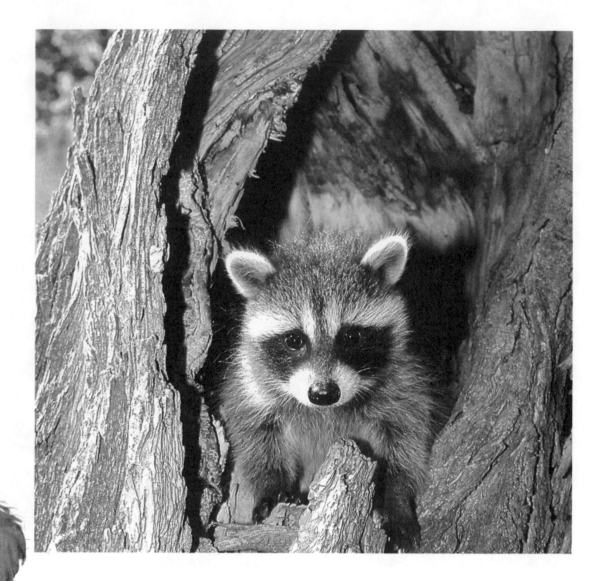

The baby raccoon can climb up
into its home in a hollow tree.

A baby deer is called a fawn.
A fawn's spotted coat helps it hide
in the grass.

A baby rabbit is a bunny. It has long
ears and a short, fluffy tail.

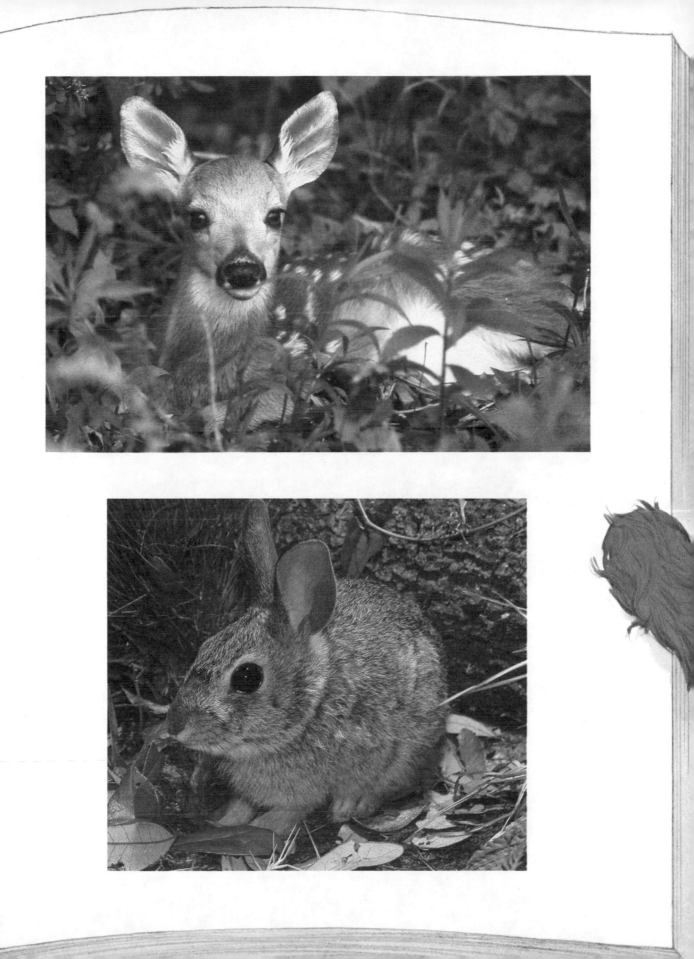

Some baby animals live on the farm.
Baby sheep are called lambs.
They have soft, woolly coats.

Many farmers raise ducks and chickens.
Ducklings are baby ducks.
They can swim and find food a few
hours after they are born.

Chicks are baby chickens.
They are covered with fluffy yellow
feathers called down.

A newborn horse is called a foal.
Foals can run on their long, thin legs
soon after they are born.

A baby cow is called a calf.
Calves often sleep in a barn on a bed
of warm, dry hay.

Baby goats
are called kids.
Goats are good
climbers.

Oh! This mother
goat has <u>two</u> kids!
They are twins.

A baby kangaroo is called a joey.
It stays in its mother's pouch until
it is big enough to get around by itself.
Joeys have large feet, a strong tail,
and are very good jumpers.

The baby koala is called a cub.
Koalas spend most of their time in trees.
The mother carries her cub until it is
almost fully grown.

Baby lions are also called cubs.
Lion cubs like to play.
They have very sharp
teeth and claws.

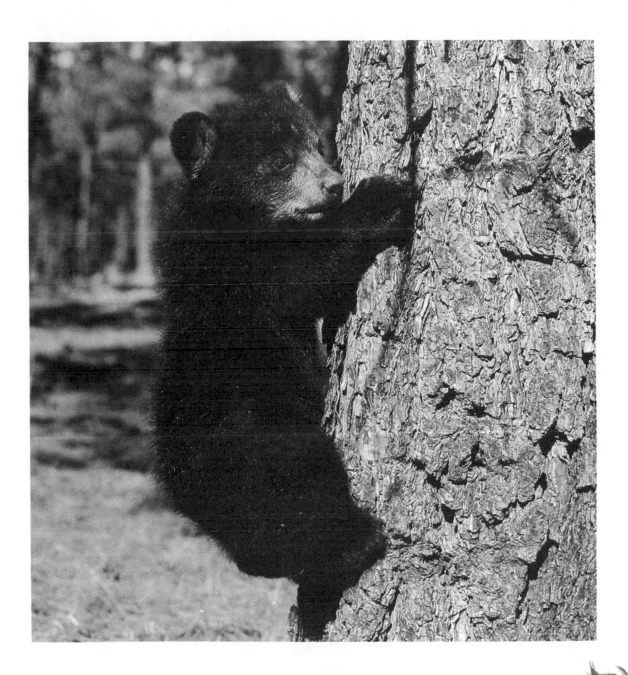

Baby bears are called cubs, too.
Bear cubs have thick fur.
Their strong claws help them
to climb trees.

A baby elephant is called a calf.
The mother elephant can use her trunk
to guide her little calf along.
Elephants can also use their trunks
to drink water or pick up food.

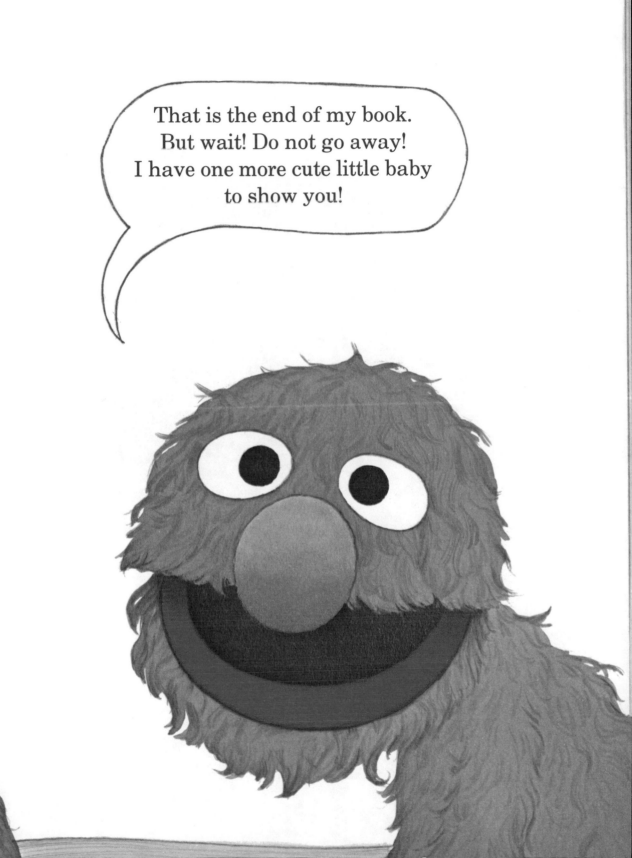

Look at this baby monster.
He is soft and blue and furry.
Isn't he cute and adorable?
I love <u>all</u> the little babies.
Do you want to read my book again?
Oh, joy! Let's start at the beginning!